First published as *The Little Dog Laughed* in 1989
by Macmillan Children's Books
a division of Macmillan Publishers Limited
Eccleston Place, London SW1W 9NF
and Basingstoke
Associated companies worldwide

This edition first published 1998

ISBN 0-333-72269-8

1 3 5 7 9 8 6 4 2

A CIP catalogue record for this book is available
from the British Library

Printed in Hong Kong

Lucy Cousins'
big book of
Nursery rhymes

MACMILLAN CHILDREN'S BOOKS

Contents

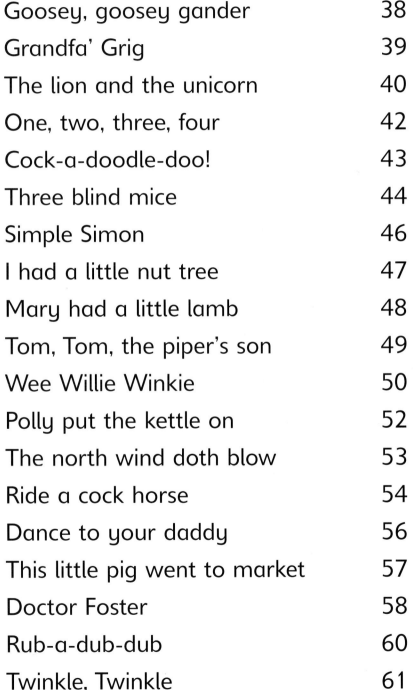

humpty dumpty sat on a Wall

Humpty Dumpty
Sat on a wall.
Humpty Dumpty
Had a great fall.
All the King's horses
And all the King's men
Couldn't put Humpty
Together again.

Baa, baa, black sheep,
Have you any wool?
Yes, sir, yes, sir,
Three bags full.

One for the master,
And one for the dame,
And one for the little boy
Who lives down the lane.

baa baa black sheep

Hickory,

    dickory,

        dock,

The mouse ran up the clock.
The clockstruck one,
The mouse ran down.

    Hickory,

        dickory,

            dock.

One, two, buckle my shoe;   Three, four, knock at the door;

Five, six, pick up sticks;   Seven, eight, lay them straight;

Nine, ten, a big fat hen;

Eleven, twelve, dig and delve;

Thirteen, fourteen, maids a-courting;

Fifteen, sixteen, maids in the kitchen;

Seventeen, eighteen, maids in waiting;

Nineteen, twenty, my plate's empty.

there was a crooked man

There was a crooked man
Who walked a crooked mile.
He found a crooked sixpence
Upon a crooked stile.

He bought a crooked cat
to catch a crooked mouse,
And they all lived together
In a little crooked house.

old mother hubbard

Old Mother Hubbard
Went to the cupboard
To fetch her poor dog a bone.
But when she got there,
The cupboard was bare,
And so the poor dog had none.

The dame made a curtsy,
The dog made a bow.
The dame said, your servant.
The dog said, bow-wow.

Christmas is coming,

The geese are getting fat.

Please put a penny

In the old man's hat.

If you haven't got a penny,

A ha'penny will do.

If you haven't got a ha'penny,

Then God bless you!

the geese are getting fat

17

Jack and Jill

Jack and Jill

Went up the hill

To fetch a pail of water.

Jack fell down

And broke his crown,

And Jill came tumbling after.

Then up Jack got

And home did trot

As fast as he could caper.

To old Dame Frown,

Who patched up his crown

With vinegar and brown paper.

Mary, Mary, quite contrary,
How does your garden grow?
With silver bells and cockleshells,
And pretty maids all in a row.

mary mary

Jack be nimble

Jack be nimble,
Jack be quick,
Jack jump over
The candlestick.

21

there
was
an old
woman

There was an old woman
Who lived in a shoe,
She had so many children
She didn't know what to do.
She gave them some broth
Without any bread.
She spanked them all soundly
And put them to bed.

Hey, diddle, diddle,

The cat and the fiddle,

The cow jumped over the moon.

The little dog laughed

To see such fun,

And the dish ran away with the spoon.

the cat
& the
fiddle

the
dish
ran away
with
the spoon

Old King Cole

Old King Cole
Was a merry old soul,
And a merry old soul was he.

He called for his pipe,
And he called for his bowl,
And he called for his fiddlers three.

his fiddlers 3

my
black
hen

Hickety, pickety,
My black hen,
She lays eggs
For gentlemen.
Gentlemen
Come every day
To see what my
Black hen does lay.

Cobbler, cobbler, mend my shoe.
Get it done by half past two.
Stitch it up and stitch it down,
Then I'll give you half a crown.

Oh, the brave old Duke of York,

He had ten thousand men.

He marched them up to the top of the hill,

And he marched them down again.

And when they were up, they were up,

And when they were down, they were down,

And when they were only halfway up,

They were neither up nor down.

the
brave
old
duke
of
York

Sing a song of sixpence,
A pocket full of rye,
Four and twenty blackbirds
Baked in a pie.

When the pie was opened,
The birds began to sing.
Wasn't that a dainty dish
To set before the King?

little
miss
muffet

Little Miss Muffet sat on a tuffet,
Eating her curds and whey.
Then along came a spider
Who sat down beside her
And frightened Miss Muffet away.

One, two, three, four, five,

Once I caught a fish alive.

Six, seven, eight, nine, ten,

Then I let it go again.

Why did you let it go?

Because it bit my finger so.

Which finger did it bite?

This little finger on my right.

The Queen of Hearts
She made some tarts,
All on a summer's day.
The Knave of Hearts
He stole those tarts
And took them clean away.

The King of Hearts
Called for the tarts
And beat the knave full sore.
The Knave of Hearts
Brought back the tarts
And vowed he'd steal no more.

Goosey, goosey gander,
Where shall I wander?
Upstairs and downstairs
And in my lady's chamber.
There I met an old man
Who would not say his prayers,
So I took him by the left leg
And threw him down the stairs.

38

Grandfa' Grig

Had a pig

In a field of clover.

Piggy died,

Grandfa' cried,

And all the fun was over.

Grandfa' Grig
had
a
pig

the lion
and the
Unicorn

The lion and the unicorn
Were fighting for the crown.
The lion beat the unicorn
All around the town.

Some gave them white bread,
And some gave them brown.
Some gave them plum cake
And drummed them out of town.

One, two, three, four,
Mary at the cottage door,
Five, six, seven, eight,
Eating cherries off a plate.

cock
a
doodle
doo

Cock-a-doodle-doo!
My dame has lost her shoe,
My master's lost his
    fiddling stick
And knows not what to do.

Cock-a-doodle-doo!
What is my dame to do?
Til master finds his
    fiddling stick,
She'll dance without her shoe.

Three blind mice,
See how they run!
They all ran after
The farmer's wife,
Who cut off their tails
With a carving knife.
Did you ever see
Such a thing in your life
As three blind mice?

Simple
Simon

Simple Simon
Met a pieman,
Going to the fair.
Says Simple Simon
To the pieman,
Let me taste your ware.

Says the pieman
To Simple Simon,
Show me first your penny.
Says Simple Simon
To the pieman,
Indeed I have not any.

I had a little nut tree,
Nothing would it bear
But a silver nutmeg
And a golden pear.

The king of Spain's daughter
Came to visit me,
And all for the sake
Of my little nut tree.

mary had a little lamb

Mary had a little lamb,
Its fleece was white as snow.
And everywhere that Mary went
The lamb was sure to go.

It followed her to school one day,
That was against the rule.
It made the children laugh and play
To see a lamb at school.

Tom, Tom, the piper's son

Tom, Tom, the piper's son,

Stole a pig and away did run.

The pig was eat,

And Tom was beat,

And Tom went howling down the street.

50

Wee Willie Winkie
Runs through the town,
Upstairs and downstairs
In his nightgown,
Rapping at the window,
Crying through the lock,
"Are the children in their beds?
For now it's eight o'clock."

Polly put the kettle on,
Polly put the kettle on,
Polly put the kettle on,
We'll all have tea.

Sukey take it off again,
Sukey take it off again,
Sukey take it off again,
They've all gone away.

The north wind doth blow,
And we shall have snow,
And what will poor
Robin do then,
   Poor thing?

He'll sit in a barn
And keep himself warm
And hide his head
Under his wing,
   Poor thing.

Ride a cock horse
To Banbury Cross,
To see a fine lady
Upon a white horse.

With rings on her fingers
And bells on her toes,
She shall have music
Wherever she goes.

to see a
fine lady

upon a white horse

Dance to your daddy,
My little baby,
Dance to your daddy,
My little lamb.

You shall have a fishy
In a little dishy,
You shall have a fishy
When the boat comes in.

This little pig went to market,

This little pig stayed at home,

This little pig had roast beef,

This little pig had none,

And this little pig cried,

"Wee-wee-wee," all the way home.

Doctor Foster Went to Gloucester

Doctor Foster went to Gloucester

In a shower of rain.

He stepped in a puddle,

Right up to his middle,

And never went there again.

rub-a-dub-dub

Rub-a-dub-dub, three men in a tub,
And how do you think they got there?
The butcher, the baker, the candlestick-maker,
They all jumped out of a rotten potato.
'Twas enough to make a man stare.

twinkle

twinkle

Twinkle, twinkle, little star,
How I wonder what you are!
Up above the world so high,
Like a diamond in the sky.